MARRIAGE MEDICINE

Marriage Medicine

THE MARITAL THERAPY FOR HEALTHY MARRIAGE

Freeson U. Eze

F. U. E. Publication

Contents

Dedicated

To God, who has blessed us with marriage, and all those facing marital struggles, I dedicate this book. Marriage Medicine is a guide to understanding and applying the principles of marital therapy to create and maintain a healthy marriage. To my beloved wife, thank you for being my partner and for being an example of true love.

PREFACE

Marriage Medicine is a spiritually compelling and informative book written to help couples understand the truth about marriage, the various issues that can arise in a relationship, and how to fix them. This book was written with the help of the Holy Spirit by an experienced servant of God and marriage counsellor. The book offers practical advice and biblical wisdom to help couples navigate the highs and lows of marriage.

Covering topics such as communication, trust, intimacy, and love, the book provides insight into how couples can strengthen their marriages and create a strong foundation for a lasting and healthy relationship. With thought-provoking questions and real-life examples.

Marriage Medicine is an invaluable resource for couples of any age, stage, or background looking to improve their relationship.

In Marriage Medicine, author Freeson U. Eze draws from the Holy Spirit, his own experiences, and biblical insight to guide couples in a marriage crisis. The book is a practical and spiritual guide for making any marriage work, offering a holistic approach to understanding the complicated and sometimes painful realities of married life.

The author provides a unique perspective on the pressures, expectations, and roles within a marriage and how to effectively manage them. He also offers strategies and tips for problem-solving, communication, and intimacy, as well as insightful advice on how to make a marriage last. Marriage Medicine is an essential read for those looking to build a strong and lasting relationship. It also covers topics such as commitment and forgiveness, as well as practical tips for couples on how to stay connected.

This book is essential for any couple looking to break free from divorce statistics and find healing and joy in their marriage. Marriage medicine will give couples the tools to understand each other better. Marriage medicine offers insight into how couples can recognise, accept, and address the issues in their relationships, while also providing practical steps they can take to fix them.

This book is a must-read for couples seeking to strengthen their connection and learn the secrets of making their marriage last so that they can experience the joyful, fulfilling relationship that God intended for them.

Introduction

The word of God is the best and most effective medicine for a healthy marriage because it all started with God.

I know there are many books on the subject of marriage, but still, I would like to add one more to the many so that anyone who has not read the rest can at least get this one.

I am not in any way saying this book is the best on the subject of marriage, but it will help in many ways if you will be patient enough to read it with understanding and an open mind.

My sincere heart desires that this book will heal marriages that are broken or are about to break up and restore relationships. And also strengthen those who are going through a tough time in their marriages, in Jesus' name, Amen.

Note that marriage is the only institution that predates sin. What I mean is that marriage is the only union that existed before Adam and Eve sinned against God. Could this be the reason Satan is waging war against marriages in this end time?

Judging by the rate of divorce in this generation, one will wonder what is going on: people no longer being faithful in their marriages, domestic violence here and there, cheating and being unfaithful to their partners, etc.

Marriage is a living thing; marriage has life; marriage can die; marriage can be sick and can be healthy; a healthy marriage can fall sick, and if not properly treated, it can become worse and die; Just as one's health needs attention, so do marriages; just as one takes care of his body, so also do marriages need care; just as when the body is sick or falls sick and requires medicine, so also do marriages or some marriages need medicine.

In this book, Marriage Medicine, we shall be looking at things that make marriage sick, unhealthy, or both, and what Marriage Medicine can do to improve the health of a marriage. That is why it is therapy for a healthy marriage.

It is also worth noting that some medications require you to eat properly before taking them, while others can treat one person but not another.

Marriage, like the body, experiences pain. In this book, I want us to look at marriage as a living organism on its own for a better understanding. We need to ask ourselves why the Bible most often uses marriage to talk about Jesus and the church. This shows the important role of marriage.

Marriage and family are global things that need maximum attention because the world is made up of nations; a nation is made up of communities; a community is made up of families; and families start through marriage. Quote me anywhere: if we could get 80% of healthy marriages in every family in the world, the world would be heaven on earth. Why did I say so? A healthy marriage will produce a healthy family lifestyle, and if parents train their children well to also produce a healthy family lifestyle, the circle continues.

The moral standard of living in almost every community, nation, and world at large is dropping drastically, and the major cause of this can be traced to unhealthy families or marriages. When a marriage is sick, the children suffer unexplainable mental and emotional heartbreak.

They are likely to have formed their mental images of how or what a marriage is in such a situation. For example, studies show that 70% of men who beat or hit their wives come from families with troubled marriages.

What it means is that those men came from families that witnessed how their own father beat up their mothers, especially in Africa.

Marriage is not for boys and girls; it is for mature adults. Mature adults here have nothing to do with age because there are so many people who are advanced in age but still behave like children.

I call them adult babies. Marriage is God's force on earth to bring part of His will to this planet. When we understand that marriage was God's plan, we can take it seriously and not joke with it.

Every person, including singles who are available for marriage, should read this book. This includes men and women. This book will be beneficial to pastors, marriage counsellors, anyone working in a marriage institute, and singles planning to marry.

Additionally, if this book was helpful to you after reading it, please tell your family and friends about it. You might be assisting someone in mending their failing union.

In Jesus' name, I pray that the Holy Spirit will assist you in understanding what you are reading and will assist those who will read this book later in resolving the problem in their marriages. Amen.

1

Part:1

Marriage: The force of God through the family

God's Master Plan for Marriage:

One of the greatest forces on earth is family, and only marriage can create a family, which makes marriage a force on earth. If everyone can understand marriage as a force of God on earth, then many people will do everything possible to handle their marriages with care.

I want to begin at the beginning because God created marriage from the beginning. I want us to understand what God did and what God's plans are for marriage and family relationships. Read what the Bible says.

"26. And God said, let us make man in our image, after our likeness; and let them have dominion over the fish of the sea, and over the fowl of the air, and over the cattle, and over all the earth, and over every creeping thing that creepeth upon the earth.

So, God created man in his own image; he created him in the image of God; he created male and female.

And God blessed them, and God said unto them, "Be fruitful and multiply, and replenish the earth, and subdue it; and have dominion over the fish of the sea, and over the fowl of the air, and over every living thing that moveth upon the earth." KJV 28:1–1:26 Genesis

"Thus, the heavens and the earth were finished, and all their host." And on the seventh day, God ended his work that he had made, and he rested on the seventh day from all his work that he had made. And God blessed and sanctified the seventh day because it was the day on which he rested from all his work that God had created and made.

KJV 3-2:1 Genesis

"And the Lord God formed man of the dust of the ground and breathed into his nostrils the breath of life; and man became a living soul. And the Lord God planted a garden eastward in Eden, and there he put the man whom he had formed."

KJV 8-2:7 Genesis.

The force of God through a family is His plan to dominate the earth through marriage and families. This means every marriage can become a family, and every family can become a community, and communities make a nation. However, it all started with God in the beginning. Without a marriage union, there is no legal family system; forget about what this generation is trying to prove, where a woman claims to be a single mother and a man claims to be a single father, and so on. The English word for a child born out of wedlock or whose parents are not married to each other still remains "bastard.

This end-time generation thought they could be wiser than their Creator; this is why God is still God, even though He has all the powers to do whatever He wants or wills. Yet, God still follows the family circle to bring salvation to humanity. Look at what God did.

God Almighty, who rules the heavens and the earth, who has all the powers at His disposal, who could just send Jesus Christ as a fully grown-up man and yet still allow Jesus to be born through a family. As a very young and newly born-again person way back, I recall reading the prophecy of Isaiah about the birth of Jesus Christ in the Bible and concluding that the virgin girl mentioned in Isaiah 7:14 had never married and would never marry. Read it below.

"Therefore, the Lord himself shall give you a sign; behold, a virgin shall conceive and bear a son, and she shall call his name Immanuel." KJV 7:14

Isaiah, another version of the Bible, says
"So, the Lord God himself will show you that he speaks a true message. Look, the young woman who has never had sex will become pregnant. She will give birth to a son. She will call his name Immanuel." EASY 7:14 Isaiah

As a young man in Christ then, I thought she would be a single mother, just as these end-time human beings are doing these last days. But no. God has to wait even though He, as God, had already seen the young virgin He wanted to use as a vessel. God waited for a man to come in search of her hands in marriage, and after the marriage rights were done, God intercepted them before they had sex with each other. Read it below.

"Now the birth of Jesus Christ was in this way: When his mother, Mary, was espoused to Joseph before they came together, she was found with a child of the Holy Ghost. Then Joseph her husband, being a just man, and not willing to make her a public example, was minded to put her away privily. But while he thought on these things, behold, the angel of the Lord appeared unto him in a dream, saying, "Joseph, thou son of David, fear not to take unto thee Mary, thy wife; for that which is conceived in her is of the Holy Ghost. And she shall bring forth a son, and thou shalt call his name Jesus: for he shall save his people from their sins. Now all this was done, that it might be fulfilled, as was spoken of the Lord by the prophet, saying, Behold, a virgin shall be with child and shall bring forth a son, and they shall call his name Emmanuel, which, when interpreted, is, "God with us. Then Joseph being raised from sleep did as the angel of the Lord had bidden him, and took unto him his wife: and knew her not till she had brought forth her firstborn son: and he called his name Jesus." KJV 25-1:18 Matthew.

If you followed the Bible verses above, you will see how God waited for Mary until she was engaged to a man named Joseph.

and I believe it was on their wedding day or party that Joseph discovered she was pregnant, and the Bible says Joseph was a righteous man, one who feared God and had regard for other people's lives.

Then her husband, Joseph, being a just man who did not want to make her a public example, decided to confine her privately. But while he thought on these things,

Joseph was planning to divorce her secretly so that the community members will not know, if not, they would disgrace her and stone her to death. Because that was the law in Israel, as Joseph was thinking about all the events, I believe he must have asked marry who was responsible for the pregnancy, but he received no explanation from her.

Or how could she prove that the Holy Spirit was responsible for the pregnancy? There was no evidence.

The Bible says Joseph was in deep thought about the whole thing—how could a virgin be pregnant? Why is she hiding who was responsible? then God had to intercept him again, this time in his dream by sending an angel to explain to him before he took his final decision.

So, the question is, why did God allow all of this to happen to two righteous people like Joseph and Mary? The answer is this: God wanted to make sure that Jesus came through a family legally married to each other; by so doing, Jesus became a person who came through a family legally married and having legal rights on earth because no spirit can live here on earth without a body.

One thing is very important in this story: Jesus became Joseph's son as viewed by the whole family and kindred of Joseph, but to Joseph, Jesus was his adopted child, and this became a legal ground for Jesus to buy us back to God as His adopted sons and daughters.

It would have been very difficult for God to accept us back as His adopted children if Joseph had not accepted to be Jesus' stepfather, taking Him as his adopted son. But as Joseph accepted, that now gives a legal ground in the realms of the spirit for God to do the same to humanity by saying, "If a human can do it, then God will do it too.

"Having predestined us unto the adoption of children by Jesus Christ to himself, according to the good pleasure of his will,"
KJV 1:5 Ephesians

"To redeem them that were under the law, that we might receive the adoption of sons."
KJV 4:5 Galatians

The Dual Personality of Humans
"26. And God said, let us make man in our image, after our likeness; and let them have dominion over the fish of the sea, and over the fowl of the air, and over the cattle, and over all the earth, and over every creeping thing that creepeth upon the earth.

So, God created man in his own image, in the image of God created he him; male and female created he them.

And God blessed them, and God said unto them, "Be fruitful and multiply, and replenish the earth, and subdue it; and have dominion over the fish of the sea, and over the fowl of the air, and over every living thing that moveth upon the earth."

Genesis1:26-28 KJV.

The Bible verses above have some deep truth about what I am talking about. We read in Genesis chapter one, from verses 26 to 28, that God created man and woman. "So, God created man in his image; he created him in the image of God; male and female created he them."

Then how come in Genesis chapter two, verse 7, the Bible says, "And the Lord God formed man of the dust of the ground and breathed into his nostrils the breath of life; and man became a living soul? What do you think happened?

If one is not careful, you may assume the Bible is contradictory. The word of God can not contradict itself because the word of God is self-sufficient, we cannot just comprehend and download what God is saying; that is the challenge. You see, what God did in Genesis chapter one verse twenty-seven was that He created the spiritual personalities of male and female in His image, which is the original copy of human race. This personality is in the realm of the spirit as God's image, so after God created that image of male and female, the Bible says God rested on the 7th day and blessed it.

Then after the resting day of God, God resumes work, but this time it was a finishing touch on what he had already begun, which was to form the physical form of man. Therefore, the Bible used this word according to the KJV: in Genesis 1 v. 27, the word used is "God created man in His image," but in Genesis 2 v. 7, the word used is "God formed man of the dust." I hope you understand the difference now. Maybe this very version of the Bible can help.

"Then God said, "Let Us (father, son, and Holy Spirit) make man in Our image, according to Our likeness [not physical, but a spiritual personality and moral likeness]; and let them have complete authority over the fish of the sea, the birds of the air, the cattle, and over the entire earth, and over everything that creeps and crawls on the earth." So, God created man in His own image, in the image and likeness of God He created him; male and female He created them. And God blessed them [granting them certain authority] and said to them, "Be fruitful, multiply, and fill the earth, and subjugate it [putting it under your power]; and rule over (dominate) the fish of the sea, the birds of the air, and every living thing that moves upon the earth."
Genesis 1:26-28 AMP.

When you look at the amplified Bible version above, you will understand what I mean as regards to God creating the spiritual side of human race and God forming the physical body that will host the spiritual personality.

Now, after God formed man, God breathed into him, and the spiritual personality of man entered the formed body of man, and man became a living soul. Could this be the reason God told Jeremiah?

"Before I formed thee in the belly, I knew thee; and before thou camest forth out of the womb, I sanctified thee, and I ordained thee a prophet unto the nations."

KJV 1:5 Jeremiah

Mark the sentence: "Before I formed you in the belly," which means that you existed somewhere, Jeremiah, and I know you there before your body was formed in your mother's womb to live on earth.

This means all humans were living or alive in the spirit even before they were born to live here on earth. So, when God created them male and female, it was their spiritual personalities that God created; later, their physical personalities were formed to house or host the spirit man.

Then in Genesis chapter 2 verses 8 and 15–17, you will notice that God formed only the physical body of man first and gave him commands and responsibilities, and God was watching how the man was doing his job. Then God took notice that the man was lonely.

Then the question is, "What happened to God's word in Genesis chapter 1 verse 27? Which said,

"So, God created man in his own image, in the image of God created he him; male and female created he them."
KJV 1:27, Genesis

The answer to that is what I have explained above: which is, God created the spiritual personality of both male and female but had to first form the physical body of the man before that of the woman. And God did that for a very good purpose. Because, assuming God formed both their physical bodies and spiritual personalities at the same time, there would have been no need to form a woman's body differently from that of a man.

There could have been nothing like magnetism or the desirability and pull a man has for a woman, or the feelings a woman has for a man.

So, for God to form the physical body of a woman, he first clarified the need to combine the body of a woman with some body parts of a man. I believe this was the basis or the source for the feelings both males and females feel for each other.

This is also another proof that when a man has feelings for a fellow man like himself, it is demonic, and if a woman also has feelings for a woman, it is satanic. Homosexuality is dirty and from the pit of hell.

See what the Bible says.

"And the Lord God said, it is not good that the man should be alone; I will make him an help meet for him. And out of the ground the Lord God formed every beast of the field, and every fowl of the air, and brought them unto Adam to see what he would call them: and whatsoever Adam called every living creature, that was the name thereof. And Adam gave names to all cattle, and to the fowl of the air, and to every beast of the field, but for Adam there was not found an help meet for him. And the Lord God caused a deep sleep to fall upon Adam, and he slept, and he took one of his ribs and closed up the flesh instead thereof; and the rib, which the Lord God had taken from man, made him a woman, and he brought her unto the man. And Adam said, "This is now bone of my bones and flesh of my flesh; she shall be called a woman because she was taken out of man. "Therefore, shall a man leave his father and his mother, and shall cleave unto his wife; and they shall be one flesh."

Genesis 2:18–24 KJV

God Made Both humans and animals With the Capacity to Self-create.

The nature of God is like this: God creates to create itself.

Remember, we are talking about marriage: God's power manifested through the family. Please note that whatever God creates, he always creates it to create itself. That is, God never does anything twice.

Note this: after God created man in His image, the one created in His image has been self-creating ever since then. So that created male and female are still in the spirit. Also, when God formed the physical body of man, He formed it in such a way that it could self-create or form other bodies by itself; that is how God made it. This is what I mean by God created humans with the capacity to self-create themselves, the ways of God are higher than ours.

God formed man from the dust and breathed into him, and man became a living soul. But when God wanted to form the body of a woman, he took the rib off the man and formed the woman, but note that God did not breathe on the woman for the woman to become a living soul.

The one time He breathed on Adam that made him a living soul, God just took it from him and used it to do what He knows best to do: that is, brought out a woman out from Adam. The Bible never said God breathed into Eve for Eve to become a living soul.

What am I saying? Understand this: God will no longer have to come and start forming men from the dust all the time, but the one time He did, He fixed the same process inside the bodies of the first man and woman He formed to self-form other bodies.

So, when a man and a woman have sex, both of them produce enough quality and quantity of a substance that forms a body, just like the substance God used at the beginning of creation, which He (God) fixed inside of them, and marriage becomes a force of God's plan. Because only a marriage relationship give a man and woman legal rights to pro-create. So In the spiritual realms, Sex outside of legally married life is fraught with judgment.

The human image is still there in the spirit world, awaiting a union that would provide it a body or a location to call home, despite the fact that humans were created in God's image and were meant to live on Earth. Therefore, consent is needed in a relationship known as marriage between men and women. In that union, a body is created that will hold the image of God. After that, when a new body materialises and dwells with an image of God that was in the spirit, they create a family.

By now, I hope you can see that marriage is a force of God here on earth. Marriage is not something one should play or joke with. Because you both carry God's image in you, and can mingle with each other and form another body that will house or host God's image here on earth.

And Satan understands how God's systems work, which is why he attacked Adam and Eve's first legal marriage system so quickly. Even at this very time, so many marriages are under attack from the pit of hell; this is the reason there are so many divorces in our generation, and many others are talking about being a single parent and the rest of it.

From the beginning, it was not so. Get this straight. Every family is a force on earth, and marriage is the fundamental foundation of it all.

Anytime Satan destroys a marriage, what that means is that he has succeeded in confusing the next generation that is to come out of that marriage or family.

I pray for you as you are reading this book that you will not destroy your marriage yourself, and may Satan never destroy your marriage in Jesus' name. And if you are currently experiencing difficulties in your marriage, may the hand of God be upon you, and may you see a solution to fixing your marriage in this book by the Spirit of God. Amen.

2

Part: 2

Just before you say these two phrases "I love you" & yes I do

It will be very good and necessary for anyone and everyone to understand these two most powerful phrases that can bring another life here on earth. Is a pity that many people have to stumble into relationships and into marriage without first-hand knowledge about what loving a person really connote.

Some stumble into a love affair with a wrong mindset of what love is, this is the reason many cannot withstand the weight of love when it becomes heavy. So many people enter a relationship with the knowledge of the sweet side of love, thinking that it will always remain sweet all the days of their life. But now you are about to see some other side of love you do not know existed.

Two Uncommon Phrases That Look Common

I love You, is a phrase that appears frequently before marriage but is always the foundation of every relationship, however it is no longer, in reality, frequent if you apprehend the deep meaning of it. And the 2nd exotic phrase that appears frequently at the beginning of a marriage or relationship is 'YES, I DO. This is (Giving your consent about the relationship)

Do you understand the true meaning of these words before you secretly say yes to him or her, before you tell your family and friends about him or her, and before you stand in front of people who will be present when you publicly and repeatedly say these words that seem common but are rare—the words that have been abused in this generation—? These are the words "YES, I DO" and "I LOVE YOU."

Do you know what love is all about? Let's avoid misusing the term "love," as 90% of people who declare their love for someone else are unaware of its true meaning. Therefore, the next time you tell someone of the other sex that you love him/her, try to grasp what love really is.

Hence, the next time you're ready to enter into a committed relationship or are not married yet, ask yourself these questions before you say these words. This is a question you should ask yourself. 1. Definition of love, 2. Is love painful or sweet? 3. How much would it cost me to fall and remain in love with him or her?

What is ' I love you? And What is Love?

Beyond the definition and meaning found in dictionaries. The meaning of the phrase "I love you" varies depending on the individual and their perception. The definition of the word "love" varies among individuals based on the circumstances and nature of the connection. While I may not address every facet of what love entails in this book, other works do.

However, examine the definition of love from this 8-standing point to have a deeper comprehension of this subject and a better understanding of what this book is discussing in this chapter.

8 Types of Love you should know and understand.

1. Philia — Affectionate love.

Philia is love barring romantic enchantment and takes region between buddies or family members. It takes place when people share equal values and admire each distinct — it's commonly referred to as "brotherly love."

How to Show Philia:
* Engage in deep dialogue with a friend.
* Be open and trustworthy.
* Be supportive in difficult times.

2. Pragma — Enduring love.

Pragma is a special bonded love that matures over many years. It is an eternal love between a couple that chooses to put equal effort into their relationship. Commitment and dedication are required to reach "Pragma." Instead of "falling in love," you are "standing in love" with the accomplice you favour by using your aspect indefinitely.

The unconscious drives companions closer to every other. This feeling comes unknowingly and feels purposeful.

How to Show Pragma:

* Continue to improve the bond of long-term relationships.

* Seek and exhibit effort with your partner.

* Choose to work with your companion no matter how difficult he or she may be.

3. Storge — Familiar love.

Storge is a natural love taking place love rooted in dad and mom and children, as nicely as nice friends. It is a countless love constructed upon acceptance and deep emotional connection. This love comes without problems and at once in guardian and toddler relationships.

Your reminiscences motivate long-lasting bonds with some other individuals. As you create extra memories, the cost of your relationship increases.

How to Show Storge:

* Sacrifice your time, self, or private pleasures.

* Quickly forgive damaging actions.

* Share memorable and impactful moments.

4. Eros — Romantic love.

Eros is a primal love that comes as a herbal intuition for most people. It is a passionate love displayed thru bodily affection. These romantic behaviours include, however, are no longer constrained to, kissing, hugging, and keeping hands. This love is a wish for some other person's bodily body.

Physical physique (Hormones)
Your hormones awaken a fireplace in your physique and should be satiated with romantic movements from an admired partner. Originally intended for couples. Not for unmarried people.

How to Show Eros:
* Admiring someone's bodily body.
* Physical touch, such as hugging and kissing.
* Romantic affection and sex.

5. Ludus — Playful love.

Ludus is a childlike and flirtatious love frequently observed in the commencing ranges of a relationship (a.k.a. the honeymoon stage). This kind of love consists of teasing, playful reasons, and laughter between two people. Although frequent in younger couples, older couples who try for this love locate a greater beneficial relationship.

The Astral (Emotion)

Your thoughts permit you to experience giddy, excited, fascinated, and worried with some other person.

How to Show Ludus:
* Flirt and interact in whimsical conversation.
* Spend time collectively to snicker and have fun.
* Exemplify childlike conduct together.
* rapid to forget about every other mistake.

6. Mania — Obsessive love.

Mania is an obsessive love closer to a partner. It leads to undesirable jealousy or possessiveness — acknowledged as co-dependency. I discover most instances of obsessive love in couples with an imbalance of love in the direction of every other. An imbalance of Eros and Ludus is the major purpose of Mania. With healthful tiers of playful and romantic love, we can avoid the damage of obsessive love.

Survival instinct
Survival intuition drives a character that desperately wants their accomplice to discover a feeling of self-value.

How to Avoid Mania:
* Recognise obsessive or possessive conduct earlier than performing upon it.
* Focus on yourself as greater versus every other person.
* Put faith into your relationships.

7. Philautia— Self-love

Philautia is a wholesome love the place you apprehend your self-confidence and do not pass your non-public needs. Self-love starts evolving with acknowledging your accountability for your well-being. It is difficult to exemplify the outbound sorts of love due to the fact you cannot provide what you do not have.

Love Catalyst: Soul

Your soul approves you to mirror your crucial wants and physical, emotional, and intellectual health.

How to Show Philautia:

* Create a surrounding that nurtures your well-being.

* Take care of yourself like a father or mother would care for a child.

* Spend time around human beings who guide you.

8. Agape — Selfless Love

Agape is the very best love to offer. It is given beside any expectations of receiving whatever is in return. Offering Agape is a selection to unfold love in any instance — which includes unfavourable situations. Agape is now not a bodily act, it is a feeling, however, acts of self-love can elicit Agape on account that self-monitoring leads to results.

Love Catalyst: Spirit

Your spirit creates reason greater than yourself. It motivates you to be kind to others.

How to Show Agape:

* Dedicate your existence to enhancing the lives of others.

* Stay aware of your movements for the appropriate of humankind.

* Offer your time and charity to any person in need.

After reading through all eight types of love above, you will agree with me that love has a price tag! And for you to say " I love you? You should understand what you are saying and also understand the implications, and then to secretly or publicly say, " Yes, I Do" means you understand the consequences.

It is so painful not to understand the meaning of "I Love You" or to venture into a relationship with the wrong mindset of what love is or what marriage is. Like it or not, marriage is far beyond sex, beauty, wealth, and so forth.

The Lord was not joking when He said,
"Therefore, shall a man leave his father and his mother, and shall cleave unto his wife: and they shall be one flesh." Genesis 2:24 KJV.

The word cleave in this verse of the Bible also means united, which means the man and the wife in the name of love, must unite and become one, what that means is, that you as a person must work hard to put up with the attitude of the other person so that the unity can flow between both of you to make you one. For that to happen, get ready to do the following.

Counting The Cost

Have you counted the cost? Because love has a price tag attached to it. After studying the meaning of love above, you will agree with me that love is deeper than what many people see it to be!

It is unfortunate that so many people enter into marriage and relationships without considering the costs; many others even went so far as to say "Yes I Do" before doing so. This does not require actual currency or money, contrary to popular belief. Material possessions and values are not the price I am referring to. It isn't the bride's price or the wedding's expenditure.

Many young men have told me that they will not get married until they have built their dream home or acquired a car. Others have stated that they will wait to get married until they have millions of dollars in their bank accounts. Some young women even have what I refer to as a "spiritual scientific eye scanner," which allows them to read a man's pocket or bank account from a distance from a distance.

All that is not counting the cost, even though one cannot neglect them, they are not the major cost to count when going into any relationship or marriage. For example.

There was a story about a wealthy king some time ago, his only son fell in love with a young lady a few years in school, and when he returned, he told his father; that he want to marry the lady. The father being a wise king told the son to wait, and that he was not yet ready for marriage but the young man kept disturbing him and saying he would run out of the kingdom with the lady if the father refused him to get married to the lady.

The father being a wise king agreed but with a condition that he (the son) will take care of a pet that he has always wanted because the boy loves pets. So, they all agree for 6 months.

The father bought a pig, and hand over to his son, to take good care of it with the condition that the pig as a house pet, should always be neat. The son was happy and started taking care of the pig, he would wash the pig, feed the pig, and do all he could by himself. But after a few hours, the pig will still run into dirty places and get dirty.

This continued for 28 days, and one day, the young man got angry and shot the pig dead, and went to his father and said, Father, the pig annoys me and I killed it. The father asks him, why? He said every time I birth the pig, it would run back into dirty places, and no matter how I fed the pig with clean plates, it would still go to feed on dirty places, so I killed it.

The father said, Son if you couldn't keep a pig clean for 30 days, then why do you want to marry? If you couldn't endure the pig for a month, how do you convince me you will endure some dirty character of your wife when you marry her? Because marriage is filled with dirty characters and attitudes that will irritate one another, and marriage is for better times and for worst of times and until death part both of you. That was when the young man understood the message.

This story is a true-life story, though it refers to an animal, but do you know that it is easier to handle animals than to handle humans? Do you know there are characters in humans that look more dirty than the dirtiness of a pig?

Secondly, age is not proof that one is mature for marriage, I have seen old people behave like children in marriage, and younger people behave maturely, the only reason God created Adam as an adult is because God wants him to handle his marriage maturely.

Read: "And the Lord God said, it is not good that the man should be alone; I will make him a help meet for him."

Genesis 2:18 KJV.

Marriage is for men and women who are mature in mind. God had all the power to create Adam as a child so he could grow, but He did not because of marriage. Man means (Mature Active Nature). While woman is (Womb man) meaning, a man that has a womb, then putting it together, it will be, (Womb of a Mature Active Nature) woman.

So, in the spirit realm, age is not measured in numbers, but it is measured in the nature and level of maturity. One may be 40 years old in numbers but acts like 14 years old in mindset and reasoning capacity (Maturity), this is the main reason, you see two adults in a marriage or relationship who cannot handle their differences, they cannot overlook the fault of the other person, which lead into a divorce. I called them (Adult Teenagers).

As a Minister of God, I have found out in my marriage counselling with some people, that some men and women are old but with a child's mindsets. They still behave and reason like children. What the king in the story in this book was trying to prove to his son was that. Marriage is for the mature mind, not a grown-up adult.

So, when I am talking about counting the cost, what am saying is this, can you accommodate the dirty side of whom you are in a relationship with or about to marry or have married?

That she looks beautiful does not mean she cannot mess up, and that he looks handsome and rich is not a guarantee that he will not behave like a child sometimes. So, in those worst of days or times when your so-called lover or partner begins to mess up, can you put up with it to withstand those days? That is part of counting the cost.

Some costs to count are

The price you pay to show your sweetheart how much you care. Anyone claiming to be a lover needs to be prepared to pay a price in order to demonstrate their sincerity. Love is all about making sacrifices; if you're not willing to do that, don't get married or enter into a relationship.

From the study about eight types of love, one thing is common among them all, sacrifice, though the sacrifice in same is louder or more visible than orders, before one can properly show or practice any type of love, there is some level of sacrifice involved.

The question is, are you ready to sacrifice some things for the love you have for your partner? You will sacrifice your time, your wealth, and your body, and your daily and everyday lifestyle will be a sacrifice because of your love for someone.

For example, if you love watching football and your wife loves movies, one person must pay the prize to sacrifice that which gives pleasure to him for the other person. If you say you will not sacrifice it, then you will have to sacrifice extra money to fix that, and that is to buy another television and other gadgets. This is still a sacrifice.

A woman has to sacrifice her beauty and get pregnant for another life to be born on earth. The sacrifice here is her physical body, almost every part of her body will be reshaped, and sometimes, some parts of a woman's body may even be damaged because of the pressure of pregnancy. It is a great sacrifice because of love.

As for men, sometimes, they sacrifice their lives by taking risks just to make their families comfortable. They inconvenient themselves for others. Love is all about sacrifice, so before you say "I love You" think again, because what you are saying by that phrase is, I am ready to sacrifice some things precious to me for your sake.

If you are not ready for such sacrifice, please stay out of marriage, if you are not ready to pay for the cost, stay away because it would be better for you.

One of the main reasons so many people divorce is that they just come to the conclusion that they can no longer afford the costs. Alternatively, the price is substantial and they are not prepared for it all.

There was a time when being married was part of the criteria for getting a job, though I do not know if that is part of it in this generation, the board of directors put it as part of their interviews because they believe if you can keep your marriage and put up with the characters of your partner, then you can put up with the attitude of people in the office you are to occupy. That was the demand of such an office.

The Story Behind Valentine

The Catholic Church acknowledges at least three exclusive saints named Valentine or Valentinus, all of whom have been martyred. One legend contends that Valentine was once a priest who served at some stage in the third century in Rome. When Emperor Claudius II determined that single guys made higher troopers than those with better halves and families, he outlawed marriage for younger men. Valentine, realising the injustice of the decree, defied Claudius and persevered to operate marriages for younger enthusiasts in secret.

When Valentine's movements had been discovered, Claudius ordered that he be put to death. Still, others insist that it used to be Saint Valentine of Terni, a bishop, who was once the proper namesake of the holiday. He, too, used to be beheaded by way of Claudius II outdoor Rome.

Other memories advise that Valentine may additionally have been killed for trying to assist Christians to break out of harsh Roman prisons, the place they have been regularly overwhelmed and tortured. According to one legend, an imprisoned Valentine, in reality, dispatched the first "Valentine" greeting himself after he fell in love with a younger girl—possibly his jailor's daughter—who visited him all through his confinement. Before his death, it is alleged that he wrote her a letter signed "From your Valentine," an expression that is nevertheless in use today. Although the fact at the back of the Valentine legends is murky, the tales all emphasise the sacrifices made for love. Though I am not in any way opposing or disproving the Feb, 14 celebrations. That is not the reason for this book. It was used right here to explain a point.

The point to note in the story and history of Valentine's Day is that they all pay a price for the love they have toward someone. The big question is still, are you ready to pay the price of love? Not this nonsense that the world is celebrating sex day in the name of Valentine's Day.

Those men in their time according to history never cared for sex, but their love was pure and sacrificial. That is why it is worth celebrating.

"Therefore, a man shall leave his father and his mother and shall become united and cleave to his wife, and they shall become one flesh. [Matt. 19:5; I Cor. 6:16; Eph. 5:31-33.]"
Genesis 2:24 AMPC.

I have a question for you. Are you willing to overlook his or her flaws? Are you ready to hate the suffering that he or she will cause you while yet loving them? If you are already married, consider all the hurts you have endured as a result of your spouse as a price you have to pay. Are you prepared to move on and let go of everything? in order for the two of you to begin again? Then keep on reading this book and your marriage will recover.

If you are already married, kindly read this book with your spouse. The two of you should honestly discuss whatever you learned from it, share your interests, and reflect on what you have gained.

If you are about to enter marriage, when you get this book, I recommend you send your partner a copy and also follow up by asking them about the chapters they read and sharing your point of view.

The law of love and marriage

"The wife hath not power of her own body, but the husband: and likewise, also the husband hath not power of his own body, but the wife."
1 Corinthians 7:4 KJV.

"I want you to live as free of complications as possible". When you're unmarried, you're free to concentrate on simply pleasing the master. Marriage involves you in all the nuts and bolts of domestic life and in wanting to please your spouse, leading to so many more demands on your attention. The time and energy that married people spend on caring for and nurturing each other, the unmarried can spend in becoming whole and holy instruments of God.

1 Corinthians 7:32-35 MSG.

But a married man has to think about his earthly responsibilities and how to please his wife. His interests are divided. In the same way, a woman who is no longer married or has never been married can be devoted to the Lord and holy in body and in spirit. But a married woman has to think about her earthly responsibilities and how to please her husband."

1 Corinthians 7:33-34 NLT

IT IS NOT ABOUT You, BUT ALL ABOUT YOUR PARTNER

The law of marriage says, I'm willing to give up some things for you, but the law of love says. I have given my all to you my spouse, and I will always be by your side. It is no longer about me.

In a marriage, your spouse comes first and not yourself. Your entire focus should be on pleasing your partner. This is the law of marriage: if you break it, you are letting the devil into your marriage. Your appearance is to please your spouse; your drinking is to please the other; your clothing, your friends, your daily routine, etc. are all to please the other.

The Bible version above says, (for the man) a married man has to think about his earthly responsibilities and how to please his wife. His interests are divided. And for the (woman) it says, but a married woman has to think about her earthly responsibilities and how to please her husband." This is the law that can keep your marriage.

Imagine the dynamics of a family where the husband strives to please his wife and the woman strives to please her husband. Tell me the entrant point for Satan?

In a marriage, your spouse comes first and yourself second. It is crucial to keep in mind that your partner is a unique person with needs, desires, and emotions of their own. The law of sacrifice serves as the foundation for the institution of marriage. For the benefit of the other, each partner should be prepared to give up their own needs and desires in some cases.

Regretfully, this is frequently not the case. Too often in marriages, each partner is simply thinking about what they want and need. A self-centered mindset is one of the primary reasons for divorce. You must be prepared to put your partner's demands ahead of your own if you want your marriage to flourish. It is this law that sustains a happy marriage.

Over the past few decades, divorce rates have been rising quickly everywhere in the world. While numerous factors contribute to this tendency, one of the primary causes is that marriages have become more about the individual than the bond or relationship.

In the past, they believed that marriage was a lifelong partnership between two individuals. These days, they frequently view marriage as a means of meeting each person's needs.

People often believe they have the right to dissolve their marriage if such demands are not satisfied. That's when one refers to themselves as single moms or dads. By God's design for marriage, this is blatantly incorrect.

We'll talk about how marriages have evolved over time in this book, as well as the reasons why divorce rates have gone up. It will also offer some advice on how to maintain a happy long-lasting marriage—if you just put what you've previously read in this book into practice. Because, if you have read this book all the way through, the advice for a happy marriage has already begun.

This Bible version clearly stated that one should be free from complications. Let's read it again. "I want you to live as free of complications as possible. When you're unmarried, you're free to concentrate on simply pleasing the master. Marriage involves you in all the nuts and bolts of domestic life and in wanting to please your spouse, leading to so many more demands on your attention. The time and energy that married people spend on caring for and nurturing each other, the unmarried can spend in becoming whole and holy instruments of God.

1 Corinthians 7:32-35 MSG.

Incorrect handling of marriage in accordance with the rules it requires might lead to issues and confusion. Marriage is an institution.

There is always one partner in a happy marriage who priorities their partner's happiness and well-being over their own. And in every marriage, that individual is the more successful one.

Furthermore, if one partner never makes amends to contribute to the sustained energy required to keep their marriage strong and alive, the person who is constantly engaged in their relationship may become weary or burned out.

One of the biggest causes of marriage failure is that each partner is more concerned with their own happiness than that of their spouse; they are constantly thinking about their own needs and wants and never give their spouse's interests or desires any thought.

If you want your marriage to be successful, you need to think about your partner first before yourself.

You must consider their needs and wants and ensure that you are doing everything within your power to meet their needs and desires. That's the only way you can have a happy marriage. Keep in mind that your spouse comes first in a marriage, not you. This is the law for maintaining the health of your marriage.

Adam was preoccupied with pleasing his wife to the point where he forgot the appearance of the fruit that God had instructed them not to eat (Genesis 3:1–8). To delight your companion, this book does not advise you to disobey God. This book strongly recommends that you be like Joseph the carpenter, who married Mary, the mother of Jesus, rather than like Adam.

In volume two of this book, we will discuss Adam's obedience to his wife and disobedience to God and what went wrong.

But for now, be Joseph, who, in obedience to the plan of God, and for the love he loves Mary, accepted her with a pregnancy he knows nothing about. When we read those Bible passages, sometimes we think it is easy to do that.

Read it again "

"Now the birth of Jesus Christ was on this wise: When as his mother Mary was espoused to Joseph before they came together, she was found with child of the Holy Ghost. Then Joseph her husband, being a just man, and not willing to make her a publick example, was minded to put her away privily. But while he thought on these things, behold, the angel of the Lord appeared unto him in a dream, saying, Joseph, thou son of David, fear not to take unto thee Mary thy wife: for that which is conceived in her is of the Holy Ghost. And she shall bring forth a son, and thou shalt call his name Jesus: for he shall save his people from their sins. Now all this was done, that it might be fulfilled which was spoken of the Lord by the prophet, saying, Behold, a virgin shall be with child, and shall bring forth a son, And they shall call his name Emmanuel, which being interpreted is, God with us. Then Joseph being raised from sleep did as the angel of the Lord had bidden him, and took unto him his wife: and knew her not till she had brought forth her firstborn son: and he called his name Jesus."

Matthew 1:18-25KJV.

By the laws of their land, Joseph is perfectly entitled to reject her and even to kill her. It was an obscenity to marry a pregnant woman at the time, but not this time. They would have stoned her with the pregnancy at that time, but now that's the norm, and they even call it the "single mother" situation. However, notice what Joseph had in mind. He intends to keep it a secret from the public, preserve Mary's life, and discreetly end the relationship.

But when God saw his heart, he had to send an angel into his dreams to talk to him about Mary and the pregnancy. The Bible says that Joseph took her in and never had sex with her until she gave birth. How many men can do that or accept it?

Here, Joseph demonstrated that he prepared for marriage with the right perspective. He is aware that in a marriage, his spouse—whom Joseph looked after—comes first and foremost.

When you get married, it is not just about you anymore. It is about your partner. For better or for worse, in sickness and in health, until death do you part, your partner is now your number-one priority. If you do not put your partner first, your marriage will be sick and may not last.

The Mind and Mental Divorce

What I refer to as "mind divorce" exists. This is an instance where one partner believes they are already divorced, even though they still share a house. However, he or she continues to stay in the marriage, perhaps due to the opinions of others, those of family and friends, or the limitations imposed on them by religion or for the sake of their children. I would argue that in Africa, mental divorce affects almost 70% of women and 15% of men. They are sick of their marriage, but for various reasons, they are unable to end it. But that was not God's intention for marriage; you are supposed to enjoy your marriage, not endure it.

When marriages end in divorce, the number one cause of divorce is selfishness. When one spouse puts their own needs above the needs of their partner, it creates conflict and resentment. This can lead to a feeling of being trapped, which can eventually lead to divorce.

If you want your marriage to last, you need to put your partner first. It is not about you anymore; it is all about your partner now. Repeat after me. It is not all about me anymore, but all about your partner.

The Danger of Falling in Love

I have heard guys say, I fell in love with her, and some ladies too say, He made me fall in love with him, etc. How wrong could it be with such a mindset?

Why fall in love without being in love or standing in love? Tate it or leave it, it is a dangerous thing to fall in love, because if you fall into something, there is every probability that you will rise from it. And whatever makes you arise from it can also make you walk away from it.

Example: If you fell in love with a lady because of her beauty and her sexy body, what happened when her beauty faded or her body changed shape? That means, as a guy, you will rise from where you fell because what made you fall is no longer there.

The same is applicable to ladies. If you fall in love with him because he is rich and has money to spend on you, what happens when things turn against him and he has no money to spend on you as before? I believe you will arise from where you fell.

My advice is: do not fall in love, but be in love and stay in love, or better still, stand in love. Because if you fall in love with someone, there are things about them or their character that you may not see because you fell. If you are down on the floor, you may not see them.

But if you are standing, you will see them and talk about it or try to address it, and you will also make your decision on time, whether to continue with the relationship or walk away. But if you continue, it shows you have seen the faults of your partner and their mistakes, but you still choose to be with them despite all their faults.

Those who stand, be, and stay in love and for love will always love their partner, no matter what; you will hardly hear them talk about divorce in their marriage. Plus, they will do everything possible to fix their relationship and will try to please their partners, just as the Bible says in 1 Corinthians 7:32–35, so their marriage can work.

After all, the Bible says, He who finds a wife finds a good thing " (Proverbs 18:22). Note this: you can't be falling and finding at the same time; you will not see the good thing you are looking for. So, you should be standing and searching before you can find it. So don't fall in love, but rather, be in love, stay in love, and stand in love.

I pray for anyone reading this book who has any marital issues in their marriage that God will heal their marriage and give them the grace to fix it by applying what they have learned through this book to their marriage, and may God touch their partner's heart too.

May the Lord bless and heal your marriage in Jesus' name, Amen.

3

Part: 3

The bitter truth or the sweet lies

Many people have made mistakes in relationships and marriage, and many more continue to make the same mistakes, which have the power to ruin and disrupt a long-term partnership. Never forget that trust is a fundamental element of marriage and relationships. In relationships, a significant foundation is shattered when there is a lack of trust. And falsehoods are the only thing that has the power to topple that foundation.

"Truth is bitter," as they say, but in my opinion, it really implies that truth is a delicious pill with a bitter coating on the outside. Anyone with enough patience may then lick the bitter substance and experience the sweetness of the truth, which is absolutely true.

This basically indicates that falsehoods have a delicious coating on the outside but a very bitter inside, because lies have a sweet coating on the outside but a really bitter inside. When one licks up that sweet side and gets exposed to the real thing, he or she is left with bitterness for a long time. And that is dangerous in marriage.

In every relationship, the tendency for lies may be higher than the tendency for truth, but the two parties involved should be the ones to determine whether truth prevails. Some lies in marriage relationships that people practice come from the following sources:

Lies from the devil

Remember that Satan's strength is in deception and lies; he used it against the first marriage, and he succeeded. The question is, will you also allow him to succeed in your relationship and your marriage? The Amplifier Bible puts it like this:.

"Now the serpent was more crafty" (subtle, skilled in deceit) than any living creature of the field which the Lord God had made. And the serpent (Satan) said to the woman, "Can it really be that God has said, 'You shall not eat from any tree of the garden'?"
Genesis 3:1 AMP

The scripture above makes it clear that Satan's strength is deceit and trickery. You will lose if you walk that hallway of deception with Satan. However, to vanquish Satan, lead him to the corridors of truth, where he is rendered helpless. Take the devil to the arena of truth, and you will watch him fall before you. Do not engage in conflict or negotiation with him in his domain.

According to the Bible, Satan is the father of deceit and a liar. One such deception that Satan tricks people into believing is that they should keep a secret from their spouse. If you do that, you've made a deal with Satan about your marriage or relationship.

Satan will advise you to keep such information to yourself in order to preserve your connection with your lover. This is a lie straight out of the bottom of the pit because no secret or lie endures forever; eventually, it will be discovered, and you risk losing your marriage or your relationship with your spouse.

A marriage or relationship breaks when there is no trust. And when your partner loses trust in you, then the relationship between you two will break someday.

Say the truth, tell your partner the truth about it all, and do not keep it secret because the truth will prevail over lies one day. It is a pity that about 60%–70% of relationships and marriages are built on the foundation of lies and deception.

Have you ever asked yourself this question? What would have happened if Eve had told Adam that she had some discussion with Satan and that she had eaten the fruits that God told them not to eat? Just imagine if Eve had done that, but what did she do? Let's find out as we read the Bible.

"And when the woman saw that the tree was good for food and that it was pleasant to the eyes, and a tree to be desired to make one wise, she took of the fruit thereof, and did eat, and gave also unto her husband with her; and he did eat."

Genesis 3:6 KJV.

Did you note that when Satan visited Eve in the Scripture above, it appeared as though Adam was not present? Eve was persuaded after their conversation. Observe that she consumes the fruit initially.

If Eve had informed Adam that the fruit came from the tree that God had forbidden them from eating, then what would have happened? Prior to handing it off to Adam. I think there was a chance Satan's plot would have failed because the Bible never states that Eve's eyes were opened when she ate the fruit; rather, it states that their eyes were opened after she gave Adam the fruit to eat. Let's read.

"And when the woman saw that the tree was good for food and that it was delightful to look at, and a tree to be desired in order to make one wise and insightful, she took some of its fruit and ate it; and she also gave some to her husband with her, and he ate."

Genesis 3:6 AMP

"[that is, their awareness increased], and they knew that they were naked; and they fastened fig leaves together and made themselves coverings."

Genesis 3:7 AMP

Did you note that Eve ate the fruit before giving it to Adam in verse six? This indicates that nothing happened during her fruit-eating experience. Perhaps she handed it to her spouse after deciding it was okay to eat.

It was when she gave Adam the fruit that the Bible says in verse seven, "Then the eyes of the two of them opened. So, she ate the fruit first; her eyes were not open, but when she finally gave it to Adam, then their two eyes opened.

This indicates that the outcome would have been different if Eve had not concealed the information from Adam. This illustrates a moral lesson: do not withhold secrets from one another. By agreeing to keep that secret, you are allowing Satan to exploit you and destroy your relationship. No matter how awful it is, expose it. Satan may tell you that this is the only long-term answer, but please do not heed his voice.

Although your partner may occasionally become irate or even attempt to end your relationship, the reality is that you have allowed the truth to surface, exposing Satan in the process.

As a result of your honesty and the solid basis on which trust has been formed, your so-called lover who stopped talking to you or took a break from you may eventually return. Sometimes others would tell him or her to return since you are reliable to go with if you could reveal such a secret.

And it will result in your partner trusting you with their life and growing in their love for you, which will strengthen your bond. But you might finally lose everything if you have the opposite opinion and continue to believe the devil's falsehoods. I heard this story many years ago about this family. The family was split up, and their marriage was ruined.

The story is about a woman and her family. This lady, before she got married to her husband, was a businesswoman, so they entered a relationship, which later led to marriage. After 25 years, they lived in a house, and the man was working and paying the house rent.

So, along the line, the man loses his job, and things become very hard for them. Sometimes the woman will bring money and give it to her husband, telling him she borrowed it from her family and friends, so the man will work out and pay. So things continue and become tough for the man and his family to the extent that they give them quiet notice to leave the property.

The man almost had high blood pressure, and the pressure was so high that he was confused. One day, as the man was using his car for a taxi, he carried a lady from the airport who is the best friend of his wife, so the lady was worried and asked why he was a taxi driver. He explained things to her, but the lady looked surprised and asked about his wife.

He said she was fine and also running around looking for where she could borrow money; the lady said borrow money? No, this cannot be true. If her friend owns the very building he says they are living in, why talk about the house rent? The man could not believe it.

So, the lady said, the only way to convince him is to call his wife. She calls his wife but asks him to be quiet. The lady calls her while the husband listens. And later that week, the man discovered that the house they had lived in for 25 years belonged to his wife.

As the story goes, the man packed up and left his wife and children behind. Afterward, the adult ones followed their father and showed no interest in interacting with her. Their marital union ended in this manner.

What can you learn about this story? Why did she keep her kept her spouse in the dark for twenty-five years? Nevertheless, having a home of one's own is not inherently terrible, so why did she withhold from him? The second question is, why did the man go? It's possible that he won't be able to trust her in the future.

This account makes it clear that Satan was the driving force behind the entire affair. Perhaps Satan suggested to her, saying, "If you tell him now, he won't be serious enough to work hard anymore, or he'll claim the house." Could you explain why she chose to keep this a secret for twenty-five years?

....

....

Please give your reason in the space.

What about those who had an affair with the sister or best friend of their wife? What about the women who slept with their husband's best friend the night before they were married? They thought it would last forever, so they kept it a secret.

What secret are you, keeping from your spouse? It will expose you and even destroy your marriage; therefore, you had better disclose it. Being truthful and true to the point of being overly sincere is the only way to foster trust.

And what about the other woman who was married a few months prior? She secured employment with a Chinese corporation here in Lagos Nigerian. The woman and her spouse are both Nigerians with dark complexions, but their eleven-month marriage ended due to an unforeseen circumstance. Her infant is completely white, has Chinese features, including eyes, and looks like a Chinese person. Her repeated insistence that she had no idea what had happened had even the doctors perplexed. Because her husband had left her at the hospital in a fit of rage, one of the doctors used his own money to have a DNA test done on her in order to uncover the truth.

It was later discovered that she had an affair just to get the job and positions she was looking for. But it was too late because the husband had to move on with another lady.

But what could have happened if she had told her husband about the affair at the beginning? The man would be angry, yes, but it will not last long because friends and family may step in to beg on her behalf, and if after everything she gives birth to a Chinese-looking baby, even the husband will remember she told him the truth about the affair.

Truth is bitter, as they said, but it is only bitter at the beginning but sweet at last; truth makes one sick so that it could bring lasting healing; truth can break a relationship so it could rebuild it for the better; truth exposes our nakedness so it can clothe and cover us perfectly; truth looks fearful but will surely put your heart to rest at last; the truth remains true any day, anywhere, anytime.

Don't tell lies to maintain a relationship or marriage; it will backfire on you and cause others to lose faith in you. Speaking the truth and not holding anything back builds confidence in your character. The devil will eventually laugh at you if you allow him to continue feeding your head with his charming lies.

Self or personal lies in a relationship

I have discovered that there are lies and deceit that some people tell themselves in relationships and marriages, which will hurt them later.

For example.

It's pleasant when guys compliment you on how beautiful or attractive you appear.

Ladies, please hear this. What the men or guys are telling you right now shouldn't get to you. You might leap into a relationship with him because you believe he appreciates and loves you. Sister, marriage is more than just a man who adores you; you two can carry on for a while. It's not a guarantee that he will tell you that once you marry him, just because you look lovely.

If you let those words sink into your heart, you may start telling yourself some beautiful, sweet lies that will hurt you later when the bitter side of the truth about marriage hits you.

You may even think that your beauty will keep him as your life partner for the rest of your life; eh, please think again. The truth is, haven't you seen another lady like you who is twice as beautiful as yourself? Tell yourself the truth. Read what the Bible says.

"A beautiful woman may not be honest. And she may not be beautiful when she is old. But all men speak well about a woman who is afraid of the Lord."
Proverbs 31:30 EASY

Don't allow them to deceive you to the point that you start lying to yourself. You must have seen other ladies comparable to you and whom you think are more beautiful than yourself if only you were able to speak the truth to yourself. The fact is, the person complimenting you on your beauty must have seen those ladies too, who are twice as attractive as you, which is not bad. Physical beauty alone does not make a character beautiful.

The Bible says beauty must surely fade away with time. Do not lie to yourself.

As a lady, do not marry him because he is calling you his angel; he may not call you an angel again after marriage.

That he is taking you out for dinner and the rest does not mean he will always do so. After you are married to him, tell yourself the truth now; do not feed yourself with sweet lies.

That he opened the car door for you today because both of you are in a relationship does not mean he will always do so. When you marry him, tell yourself the truth.

Sister, you want to marry him because he's amusing. It's not a guarantee that a comedian will make you laugh when you marry him or feel content all the time. It's possible that you fall in love with him because he made everyone in the room laugh, but that doesn't mean happiness and laughter will fill your home. You two will work things out in marriage.

I have seen ladies who marry comedians cry and leave their marriage.

What makes you desire to marry that individual?

What qualities in him or her drew you to pursue a romantic relationship with them? Quit lying to yourself; marriage encompasses more than that. A woman once said that if love is blind, marriage will open your eyes.

As a lady, your reason for accepting him may be a lie; you lied to yourself. The names he calls you may change when you get married to him; money is not marriage; and beauty fades away with time.

As a young man, do not marry for beauty, because beauty will fade with time, but the person will still be with you even after beauty has faded away. Sir, as the saying goes, the beautiful ones are not yet born. The Bible says.

"A beautiful woman may not be honest. And she may not be beautiful when she is old. But all men speak well about a woman who is afraid of the Lord."

Proverbs 31:30 EASY

Beauty fades away with time. Do not be deceived; tell yourself the truth, sir. That she looks sexy today does not mean she will remain like that for the next ten or fifteen years; her body shapes that draw your attention to her today will change even with just one pregnancy. Tell yourself the truth.

Tell yourself the truth, sister. Just because he is rich and handsome does not mean he is rich enough to love you. and being handsome physically does not mean he will be like that on the inside to overlook your little fault in the future after you marry him.

Marriage is a different ball game. When you are outside marriage, you may see the fault of those who are in the game, but wait until you join the game. Do not be deceived either; there is no perfect marriage anywhere on earth; it is in the hands of both people who are married to make their marriage a perfect marriage on earth.

The Deception of Sex and Gift.

The seductive power of gifts and sex has tricked a lot of people, all in the name of love. To be clear, love is not about sex, and sex is not love. Never fall for a trick or allow someone to take advantage of you by leading you to believe that a gift or a sexual encounter constitutes love. Nevertheless, both are involved in love.

So many women have been deceived by the gifts men keep giving them; in their minds or their subconscious, they may start feeding themselves lies, thinking that the man giving them the gift loves them more. The Bible is very clear on this issue.

"Thou shalt not wrest judgement; thou shalt not respect persons, neither take a gift: for a gift doth blind the eyes of the wise, and pervert the words of the righteous."
Deuteronomy 16:1 KJV

A great number of young women lost their purity as a result of accepting gifts from men. The Bible claims that a gift will cause blindness, but I contend that a gift might cause you to begin believing falsehoods to be true and feeding yourself with them. When you accept gifts from men as a lady, you will eventually lose your willpower. Your conscience will also start feeding your heart with false information, believing that you owe him one. This could lead to you offering him sex in exchange for all the gifts you have received.

According to the Bible, receiving a gift can cause someone to make incorrect judgments, even about themselves. For example, it can cause a woman who often makes accurate judgments about sin and righteousness to begin questioning the good deed she has been doing all along. It obliterates the heart's ability to discern between beautiful lies and the truth.

Approximately 70% of women in this generation have already given up their chastity to any man who can afford to buy them. We shouldn't discuss people who lost their virginity because he gave them an expensive present. though I am not advocating against receiving gifts. but am trying to explain it through the lens of love, marriage, and relationships.

Once a Lady receives a gift from the opposite sex her mind will begin filling itself with sweet lies as soon as they receive a present like that, believing the donor to be in love with her. Gifts have caused a great deal of young women to miss out on possible partners and marry the wrong person.

Many women ridiculed and laughed at the man who was meant to marry them because he was not financially secure when they first met, while another devil in human form had some money to spend on them. As a result, they failed at getting married, but later in life, they realised that they had turned down the real man because he could not afford the gift at that time.

One man once told a woman that she should never turn down a man with a vision for a man with a television because if you do, you will eventually have to watch the man whose vision you turned down on your television.

The Power Behind Gift-giving

Young, single women who hope to marry in the future should consider the following advice

When building yourself as a girl, avoid having the mentality that "use what you have to get what you want." Instead, be honest with yourself and stay on the correct path. It is an incorrect perspective.

Ladies, especially those who are single, should learn how to say no. Make every effort to acquire the skill of saying no; it will benefit you and make men respect you more. Know when to refuse a certain present from a man because it may be a trap. Saying no thank you will confuse the fraudsters who prey on young women about your personality type; therefore, learn to say no thank you.

Because the gift's power is only released when you say "yes" or take it from the giver, you must learn to say no. Due to their long-standing habit of accumulating presents from men, many women cheat on their spouses even after being married. Despite being married.

They continue to receive gifts from men, even after getting married, including from their former lovers before they got married.

Growing up in the "80s," one of the things that kept young ladies saved was their ability to say no and reject gifts from the opposite sex. This is a virtue that has been lost with this new generation.

When you, as a lady, keep accepting gifts from men', you are opening yourself up to assault unknown to you. Remember, there is a saying that goes like this:.

The hand of the giver is always above the receiver. Meaning, the one who is giving you has the upper hand.

This is important to know, young lady: if you don't like him or want him, don't get anything from him. If you do, he will have the upper hand, and the gift's power will be released into the spirit world. Then, your conscience and heart will deceive you as well and force you to pay him back with sex—something you were not ready to do.

Sometimes it would be nice to believe that gifts are genuine tokens of affection, given without any expectation of recompense. (Indeed, the Merriam-Webster dictionary defines "gift" as something "voluntarily transferred" and "without compensation.") But if you have ever had the niggling sense that something other than selflessness drives the giver, then think again. Though gifts are not wrong on their own, it all depends on the giver and the recipient. And the motive behind their action.

There's a whole lot behind gift-giving that goes very close to the basics of living together." Gift-giving, after all, is a physical symbol of a personal relationship and an expression of social ties that bring individuals together. Note the word "that brings individuals together.".

A gift is then symbolic of the perceived value of the relationship, and, to prevent any strain or awkwardness, gifts must be repaid in some way. This means that giving a gift inevitably creates debt in the conscience of the recipient. "There's a debt balance that people keep, silently, with each other, within their hearts in relationships," especially with the opposite sex, which demands repayment in one way or another.

This gift exchange can be summarised by the Latin phrase Do Ut des: "I give because I expect you to give something back."

That is why most times some guys, genuinely without any interest in mind, start giving a gift to a lady, but down the line, because a gift also has a stronghold in the spirit, the power behind it can be activated, which may result in a negative or positive impact because the gift has both in the spirit realms. The next thing you will notice is that the guy starts feeling like the lady owes him some debt that she needs to pay back, and the lady on the other side may feel indebted to him too.

I recall the introduction of BlackBerry phones to Nigeria between 2002 and 2007. The Bold2 phone type was very popular at the time, and many young women wanted to use it at all costs. As a result, wicked guys started giving young girls phones. As I found out, in certain instances, the women came by themselves to give themselves to the man who gave them bold2. At the time this book was written, the phones being used as beats were the iPhone 11, 12, 13, 14, Promax, etc.

Many young women in those days were pregnant as a result of bold2, others were deflowered, and some were raped but were unable to speak out or file a report to obtain justice since they had obtained bold2 from the male. What about the large number of young women who get married "by force"? Despite their lack of preparation for the marriage, they couldn't resist because they had accepted the gift from that man.

How about giving birth to unwanted children, children that they were not prepared for? What about those who die because they got pregnant and wanted to abort it, but things became complicated and they lost their lives? Some have damaged their wombs. Tracing all this back is accepting gifts from men.

I am not saying taking gifts is a sin, but learn to say no as a lady' it will make you stronger and men will never toil with you, but you can accept gifts from the person you are sure that he wants to marry you and you also like him and want to spend the rest of your life with. In such cases, accept what he gives you.

Do not be one of those who will always say, "He Used Me and Dumped Me.".

Sex as a reward

To the men, do not fall victim to this. Women these days see sex as a reward for men; they believe that when you have sex with them, they have paid you, maybe as the result of all you have been doing for them. By giving you their body, they try to clear their conscience of the silent debt for all the gifts or help you have rendered. What both do not know is that a relationship goes beyond sex and gifts, and marriage is far more than all that. Do not be deceived.

To all men: please be mindful of the gifts you offer to the opposite sex, as your generosity and concern for her will instill a debt conscience in her. In other words, the more you take care of and give gifts to a woman who is not your sister, mother, or other family member, the more that generates a sense of obligation in her, or perhaps the idea that you are expecting something in return. These phenomena are psychological in nature.

After a while, she begins to experience sentiments and emotions that develop into what I refer to as mushroom love and a burning desire to please you, the guy. At that point, you will notice some odd behaviour whenever she is in your presence if you are a sensible guy and you do not have any bad intentions for all the gifts and care you have given her. As a male, you have to flee for your life at this point, or you will succumb to sexual immorality.

The truth is that, in the beginning, none of you planned it that way, but the power of sex as a reward must surely come into play. So, it is now left for both of you to decide, or for you, as the man, to make your decisions.

Gift-giving here refers not only to cash or the buying of gift items, but it also refers to little kindness shown to a lady, any care or act of kindness of any sort.

This was the major challenge Joseph in the Bible had, the Bible said!!

"Now his master saw that the Lord was with him and that the Lord caused all that he did to prosper (succeed) in his hand. So, Joseph pleased Potiphar and found favour in his sight and he served him as his personal servant. He made Joseph overseer over his house, and he put all that he owned in Joseph's charge. It happened that from the time that he made Joseph overseer in his house and [put him in charge] over all that he owned, that the Lord blessed the Egyptian's house because of Joseph; so, the Lord' S blessing was on everything that Potiphar owned, in the house and in the field. So, Potiphar left all that he owned in Joseph's charge; and with Joseph there he did not [need to] pay attention to anything except the food he ate. Now Joseph was handsome and attractive in form and appearance. Then after a time his master's wife looked at Joseph with desire, and she said, "Lie with me." But he refused and said to his master's wife, "Look, with me in the house, my master does not concern himself with anything; he has put everything that he owns in my charge. He is not greater in this house than I am, nor has he kept anything from me except you, because you are his wife. How then could I do this great evil and sin against God [and your husband]?" And so it was that she spoke to Joseph [persistently] day after day, but he did not listen to her [plea] to lie beside her or be with her." Genesis 39:3-10 AMP

This was the major issue Joseph faced in that house. Joseph does everything in the house very perfectly; when madam says Joseph cleans the house, he will clean it very fine to her test or far beyond. When she says Joseph cooks, he will do it with so much passion and perfectly, and it pleases her so much that she wants to reward him, but everything—the bank account, clothes shop, shoe companies—that she and her husband own has been placed under Joseph. He was in charge, and the whole thing in her now grows into the power of sex as a reward. Sex as a reward could be misunderstood, and one may think she is in love.

Sex as a reward became such a burning passion in her that she must do it at all costs. This was the reason Potiphar's wife did what she did. She was overwhelmed by the power of sex as a reward. And I believe she must have thought she was in love with Joseph, or she must have told Joseph she loved him. Just like some ladies do, when a guy spoils them with a gift and care, they grow feelings for him and think it is love. My dear, marriage is far beyond feelings; it is when you enter that you will understand.

This power of sex as a reward has been the major reason that even pastors and ministers of the gospel fall into fornication and adultery. This power is also what makes a housemaid or houseboy have affairs with their boss.

According to research, the power of sex as a reward accounts for 70% of men who sleep with or have sex with their housekeeper, office secretary, or sister-in-law who stays with them. These women were overcome by the power of sex as a reward, even though it was never their goal. they want to thank the man with sex because he provides them with a lot of care. And they blamed the devil for anything that goes wrong or if they were caught in the act, not realising that the power of sex as a reward was actually responsible.

Check it again, especially when a man is too good to ladies and shows care and gift-giving with no evil intentions at the beginning, but the more it continues, the ladies now feel like they owe him something, and the only thing she has to pay with is her body, and all this was a lie from Satan, the master of all lies.

The Bible says Satan is a liar and the master of lies.

"You are of your father the devil, and it is your will to practice the desires [which are characteristic] of your father. He was a murderer from the beginning and does not stand in the truth because there is no truth in him. When he lies, he speaks what is natural to him, for he is a liar and the father of lies and half-truths."

John 8:44 AMP

Satan is the master of deception and lies; the Bible says he was a liar from the beginning; the Bible even says Satan was a murderer from the beginning. What does that mean? It means Satan kills from the beginning through lies and deceptions. If you remember how Satan lied to Eve and, by so doing, brought death to humanity,.

"When Adam sinned, sin entered the world. Adam's sin brought death, so death spread to everyone, for everyone sinned."

Romans 5:12

This verse explains to us that Adam made a choice, and this choice brought sinful nature to humans. How did it happen? Satan deceived Eve, then Eve gave Adam the fruit without informing Adam where the fruit came from, and Adam ate the fruit. The subject matter here is deception, and Satan is behind it all.

As a man, do not fall victim to this; sex is not love, and love cannot be sex. Ladies are out there with the wrong mindsets, thinking sex is a reward.

That is why we always hear some ladies say, I gave you what you wanted, and you gave me what I wanted. Or you will sometimes hear ladies crying; he used me and dumped me.

One of the reasons is that she thought that because she rewarded him with sex, he would love her and marry her, or he would never look for another lady. Hear this again: sex cannot keep a man, especially when the man lacks self-control and discipline. Sex is not marriage, and marriage is not sex, even though sex plays a major role in marriage. You can keep your marriage healthy through sex, but you cannot keep a man or tie a man with sex.

Force yourself to accept the truth at all cost

In conclusion, you have to force yourself to accept the truth, no matter how bitter it is, because behind the bitterness of truth is hidden the sweet side of it. No matter how painful or hurtful the truth looks, it will surely prevail.

You just have to be truthful with yourself; tell yourself the truth. Do not lie to yourself because maybe it favours you today, but there is no guarantee it will favour you tomorrow. Anything built on lies will only survive a little while; it will not last, especially in marriage and relationships.

Have you ever considered why and how the older generation marriage managed to survive in the face of overwhelming adversity? In contrast to our generation, they had no marriage counsellor, but since they stood up for the truth and based their relationships and marriages on it, they served as counsellors to themselves. Unlike this packaging-obsessed generation, there is nothing to conceal, nothing to lie about, and no time for packaging.

Like this story, I heard about a marriage that lasted for only twenty-four hours.

The story is about a young man who was in a relationship with a lady for seven years plus. Finally, they decided to marry themselves, and after the wedding in 2018 or so, that same Saturday night as new couples, the young man wanted to have sex with his wife. It turned out to be dramatic.

For more than 7 years of her life, the lady has been living in lies; she wears artificial breasts because her real breasts are small, and she also wears artificial buttocks. So, the young man thought what he used to see about the lady was real, and he fell for it. So that night, when the lady zipped up and removed all the packaging, the young man got angry and left the room.

The next thing he did was to call the pastor and family members. After explaining things, he asked for a divorce, saying the marriage was standing on deceit. The pastor was now asking for advice on how to handle the issue. The young man refuses, and they divorce.

They wed on Saturday, and their marriage broke up that same Saturday night, by Sunday morning, the lady was back to her parent's house.

The question now is, who is fooling who? And who lied to who? And who suffered most among the two? And as a pastor or marriage counsellor, what will be your advice to the young man not to divorce his day-old wife?

Tell yourself the truth: marriage is more than beauty and shape; some ladies are spending money to package themselves (their bodies). One bitter truth most young ladies will not want to hear is this.

Instead of spending 100% of their time and money on their outlooks, spend 70% of their time and resources on your inner look and 30% on your outlook. Then you will see how God will bring a man who will marry you and spend 100% on your outlook because he has seen all the qualities he was looking forward to in a woman in your inner personality.

Invest in your inner personality, read books, build a strong good character, teach yourself to be disciplined, learn to say no, reject some gift from men, etc.' When a man sees these things in you, he will pay any price to get you as his wife.

Do not ever be a lady when your man talks about business; you do not have any ideas to contribute; he talks about work challenges; there are no solutions or suggestions from you; and the next thing you will ask him is for money for your hair or cream. Check it yourself. If you were in his shoes, how would you feel?

Young lady, invest in yourself. Marriage is more than a wedding, more than sex, and more than "I love you." Marriage is also more than I am beautiful, which is why he is dying for me. My dear, if love is blind, marriage will open his eyes and your eyes too, because some people may take it easy with you when you are not yet married to them; they may overlook certain things from you, but when you are married to same people will not take it again. That is why I say that if love is blind, as they say, marriage will open your eyes.

4

Part: 4

The Mystique of a Successful Marriage

The magic, or the miracle (depending on your point of view), of the past generation of men and women who kept their marriages and homes against all odds.

If you want to keep your marriage strong, then continue reading this book! The past generations had some pretty ingenious tricks up their sleeves when it came to keeping their marriages strong or lasting.

But the best part is that you can use these same tactics to keep your relationship working today. Find out how to make your relationship work as it was back then in the 1900s by applying a few of these tips, as well as modern tips from experts and biblical truth.

In this chapter, you will understand why and how. Even as I study and do research on how the people of old kept their marriages against all odds, some of them had issues in their marriages; some married the worst of men or women, yet they kept their marriages without divorcing.

I have always asked myself, "How did the people of old keep their marriages? Some did not know who they would marry until the day of the wedding, and yet their marriages lasted till death did them part. So many of them married partners chosen by their parents—that is, they married someone against their will or permission; this alone put off some marriage counselors' theories and advice.

I have read and heard many of them say, "Marry your friend," "Marry someone you are compatible with," etc. But what happens after many keep up with such wonderful advice from expert marriage counselors yet end up in divorce? It is a surprise to me.

I came to this conclusion while writing this book by doing personal interviews, asking the older generation directly, and doing research on them. I realised that some individuals did not marry their friends and that some did not even love the person they married at first, but they eventually grew to love them. As I previously stated, some of them went on to marry the worst possible men and women, and some of them were successful in their marriages despite not giving their approval.

Some of them marry Satan in human form and still leave peacefully without divorce.

The big question is:

What was the magic?

What did they know and do, that the current generation does not or does not recognise?

I will try my best, with the help of the Holy Spirit, to address a few of the many questions as I understood them, both through research and with the help of the Spirit.

In this chapter, we will look at what makes a marriage last and what keeps two people in love despite all odds. Some of the magic is not limited to these.

The marriage lifeline (communication)

Communication is a lifeline for any and every relationship, as well as one of the major keys to a lasting relationship or marriage. This works like magic, or a miracle, for those who understand and practice it.

Communication is essential for survival; almost every living thing communicates in some way; even a newborn baby uniquely communicates with his mother. The animals understand how to communicate with their kind.

However, there's more to this than meets the eye. The way you present your message to your spouse is just as important as what you have to say to them. Even though saying "I am sorry" is a key ingredient in marriage and any relationship, there are ways and means, including physical expression and actions, that one can use to say "I am sorry" that will still provoke their spouse. I hope you understand.

Advice from a relationship expert Consider these three Ts: text (what you will say), time (when you will say it), and tone (how you will express your words).

Another expert, Shannon, advises asking yourself three questions before bringing up a contentious subject with your spouse: "Is it true? "Does it build up?" Is it correct? She advises you to pray for God to give you the appropriate tone to use when speaking with your spouse and to think about the best moment to do it.

For example.

If something goes wrong or he does something you do not like, the best time to discuss it is not when he is watching a football game, that is, if your husband is a football lover. Instead of discussing the issue, discuss a football game with him. Ask him about the game and which team he supports, then maybe support the other team and maybe suggest a bet, like "I bet you my team will win this game. Let's bet: if your team wins, I will give you hot sex, etc., but if my team wins, you will cook dinner, or you will pay me this amount for my cooking, etc.

Then, after the game, when he is calm or you have paid him the bet, that is, if his team won, you can now discuss that issue with him. I guarantee you that he will give you the best attention you have ever received.

But if you do the opposite, he may even dress and leave the house for you, perhaps going to a bar or club to watch the game peacefully with friends. If you do that as a wife or push him out of the house, you may end up pushing him into the hands of another woman or bad friends that will influence him negatively. Believe it or not, many women have lost their husbands to this simple act.

I know of so many women who came for prayer and counseling about how their husbands are not always available or give them attention. After questions and answers, I discover they push him away by themselves. Do not forget about what the Bible says.

It is better to live in a corner of the housetop [on the flat roof, exposed to the weather] than in a house shared with a quarrelsome (contentious) woman.
Proverbs 21:9 AMP

If you understand what the Bible says here, you will stop quarreling and learn about communication so that you will not expose your spouse to the bad weather, the word "weather" in this verse is talking about bad friends that are capable of teaching him how to womanise, drink, or cheat.

To the men, there are bad friends who can influence her to consider becoming a single mother by divorcing you, the husband, you need to give her your full attention so you do not lose her too.

Communicate with your spouse in a way that is respectful and understandable. Be honest and do not play the passive-aggressive game with your spouse, expecting him or her to just know why you are upset or when you are pleased by something that he or she did or did not do.

Another tip for communicating better with your spouse is for both of you to be present in the conversation. You do not want to be half-listening while mentally reflecting on your to-do list, berating your head on your phone or laptop, or planning what you want to say while your spouse is speaking.

"Communication is the mortar that holds a relationship together," says relationship expert Dr. Amy Bellows. "If it breaks down, the relationship or marriage will crumble, and your marriage will become sick or enter coma mode. When spouses no longer communicate well, the marriage starts dying, and it nurtures no one. "It is no longer a marriage."

The voice of your body

Body language is another tip we must all pay attention to. So many people do not pay attention to it, but the truth is, that your body has a loud voice that is talking even when you are not speaking with your voice. And this body voice has destroyed many marriages and cordial relationships. Take, for example, have you ever been happy, perhaps singing and playing music, but then you saw your spouse or someone you love from afar, and he or she didn't say anything, but his or her frowning face immediately changed your mood?

That is what I am referring to. They say that actions speak louder than words, right? I have seen and heard how a husband slaps his wife, and when people ask why, what did she do? You will hear the wife say, "I did not say anything, nor did I do anything, and he just slapped me," and at that point, most men will not be able to explain the reason he slapped her. The truth is, it was her body language that made him slap her.

Although I do not condone a husband beating his wife, this is a common occurrence in marriage and relationships. I call it the silent voice that can destroy relationships. The voice of your body also speaks; that is why it is called body language.

If your marriage has lasted at least three years or less, you can look at your spouse and understand their mood without saying anything. This voice can also be heard in family circles.

When I was growing up with my family when a visitor came to the house, my dad would only look at me, and I immediately understood what he wanted me to do. Though he did not say anything, I understood what he was saying. If this can be true in a father-son relationship, it should be much more so in a husband-wife relationship.

I saw it among my parents. My dad will look at my mom, and without saying a word, she understands what he says. My mother will respond in kind, and my father will understand what she was saying or wanted to say.

As you can see, communication is not only through words; you can communicate without saying a word. Do not apologise to your spouse while your body is screaming, "You are stupid!" If the two do not match, that apology will not be accepted.

This is the reason why the other partner refuses to accept the apology, and sometimes they cannot explain why. When asked by a third party, and you start hearing the other say, "I have apologised to him, yet he refuses to accept it.
The question is, were the two communication channels we have talked about involved and present in the way you were communicating with him or her?

The truth is that we know these things but turn blind eyes and deaf ears when it comes to marriage and relationship affairs. Read the Bible verse below.
"A soft, gentle, and thoughtful answer turn away wrath, but harsh, painful, and careless words stir up anger."
Proverbs 15:1 AMP

Can anybody be angry and thoughtful at the same time? The word thoughtful in this very verse of this version of the Bible makes it clear that to be thoughtful, it will require your body composition and the posture of your body system before one can be thoughtful enough to give a soft and gentle answer to an angry partner.

I am sure by now we all agree that communication is one of the lifelines of any relationship or marriage, and talking, listening, and "mirroring back" to your spouse are effective ways to keep healthy communication flowing between you both, which in turn keeps your marriage healthy and strong.

Love the person you marry

This is a spiritual law of love, and it is one of the mysteries of the ancient people's successful marriages: they did not marry the person they loved, but they loved the person they married. This is one secret truth that our generation is attempting to brush under the rug, but it has been the secret of successful marriage for centuries.

It is in marriage relationships that I notice that love can grow cold. and the person you once loved now looks like a stranger to you.

If you marry someone you love, what you do not know is that people change through time and season, and the environment also affects people's lives. As I always say when I am speaking about marriage in conversations, "love will push both of you to enter into commitment; love will lead you to the altar for a life-time commitment; and when both of you are joined together, love will now leave both of you and stay outside the house watching how you handle yourself.

It will only take a moment for love to leave both of you and stay outside the house, watching how you handle yourself. It will also take someone among you to invite love back in.

This is why I said, "Do not marry the person you love; you must love the person you marry." While there is nothing wrong with marrying the person you love, it should not be the foundation of your marriage because there will come a time when you will not see any reason to love the person you marry, even though it is expected that you do.

This was also the ancients' marital success; This is why they could stay and marry the person chosen by their parents; this is why a lady will marry a man she has never seen before until the day of their wedding, and they never divorce.

However, some marriage counsellors of our generation used to advise, "Marry who you love," but now I advise, "Love who you marry." The idiom "for better or worse" or "in good health and sickness" can only be fulfilled at that point.

Although there is nothing wrong with such advice, some marriage counsellors in our generation used to advise, "Go into a courtship with the person you want to marry." But how do you explain couples who dated for 11 years before getting married, only to have their union end after 3 years?

How can you compare the past generation, who did not even know the person they wanted to get married to, and after their parents agreed and made all arrangements, they informed the couples of their wedding date and wed them, and they never broke up? Please ask your marriage counsellor to explain.

You see, love is a command; we are expected to love. Sometimes, however, we choose who to love and choose to ignore others, which is against God's will. Just as I wrote in the other chapter, women have no business loving their husbands; it is the business of the man to do the loving while the women do the submission; this is a law of the spiritual realm.

The problem is that we are trying too hard to do the opposite, and that will never help, no matter how hard we try. Humans have always attempted to change God's laws and principles. God told the woman to submit to the man; special marriage counsellors said to love the man.

Follow these principles, put them into practice, and watch your partner change and your love grow as it always has.

5

Part: 5

The Many Sides Of Love In Marriage

Never forget that you are not alone as you traverse the many happy and difficult aspects of married love.

Marriage is a journey with highs and lows. You will feel as though you are wading through a river of pain at times, as well as during periods when you are floating on a cloud of ecstasy. It is important for you to remember that in these later times, you are not the first, you are not the last, and you are not alone.

Marriage is a beautiful thing. It is the union of two hearts, two minds, and two souls becoming one. But like anything else in life, it is not always easy. There will be times when you will hurt each other, when you will argue and fight, and when you will want to give up.

But do not give up. Remember why you got married in the first place? Remember the love that brought you together? It is that love that will see you through the tough times if you both can hold on to it. Read what the Lord Jesus said about not holding or remembering your first love.

But I have this complaint against you. "You don't love me or each other as you did at first!"
Revelation 2:4 NLT.

This means it is a very dangerous thing to forget about how both of you started your marriage. It is very important to always keep that fresh in your mind.

There is no such thing as a perfect marriage, but with love, patience, and understanding, you can overcome anything. These three words—"love, patience, and understanding"—are the major keys that make some marriages look like they are perfect and if you can apply them to your marriage too, you will get the same results other couples have gotten over the years.

There are millions of couples who have gone through the same thing your marriage is going through. They have navigated the painful side of love and marriage and come out the other side stronger than ever. So do not give up, because your marriage is worth fighting for. Remember, life itself is based on the combination of both sweet and bitter; life is beautiful when it shows multiple colours.

Understanding the painful side of love in marriage

Remind yourself that you are not alone while you work through the difficult aspects of married love.

Every marriage has its ups and downs, and sometimes the suffering seems unfathomable. It is crucial to keep in mind that you are not experiencing this alone. Numerous pairs are experiencing the same problem.

Discuss your feelings with your partner. There is no other way to make sure you both know what is going on. Keeping your emotions inside can only make matters worse, so don't do it.

And do not be afraid to seek help from a professional if things get too tough. There is no shame in admitting that you need help. Even as you seek help from professional marriage counsellors, do not forget that God is the best of them all. Seek God and His counsel in your marriage because He is the one who instituted marriage. And before you seek help from outside, make sure, first of all, that you have been able to keep the three most important words I mentioned earlier. These words are understanding, patience, and love.

Understanding the word "understanding" in marriage

So many people claim they understand the word "understanding," not knowing that the word "understanding goes beyond its English meaning. When it comes to marriage and relationships, understanding plays a major role. Below are some words one needs to know about understanding.

According to Pastor Chris Royalseed, understanding is the combination of two words, which are,

1. Under
2. Standing

He said that for couples to really understand the word understanding, when one is standing, the other should be under, and when the other is under, the other person should be standing. He said both should not be standing or under at the same time; it will cause misunderstanding.

Understanding in marriage says, "I know you are not perfect, but I choose to stay with you and put up with all of your imperfections."

In marriage, understanding means forcing yourself to love him or her with every ugly side they have and trying your best to bring out the best in their ugliness. The ugly side here may refer to your spouse's character, behaviour, and attitude.

Understanding means having the capacity to accommodate another person the way they are and not forcing them to change to whom you want them to be but helping them to change for the best of themselves in God's picture. That is understanding.

Understanding in marriage entails being aware of your partner's flaws yet continuing to live with them as though they are flawless since your feelings for them are greater and louder than those flaws. That's understanding.

Understanding in marriage also means overlooking the faults of your spouse, never holding anything against them, and still loving them despite all their faults.

Understanding means accepting your wrongs when your spouse tells you about them and not trying to convince yourself or cover them up with one excuse or another. And assure them that you will work on improving so that you can be a better person who they will want to live with.

To have understanding is to make an effort to see things from your spouse's perspective and to honour it. Sometimes giving up your position may be costly in the short term, but in the long run, you never know when your argument will be proven correct. That's understanding.

The role of patience in marriage

When you are patient with your spouse, it appears to others that your marriage is flawless from a distance. Putting on patients as garments is my counsel to everyone who is already married or is considering marriage.

To the married individuals: I beg you, married men and women, to consider why physicians refer to the ill individuals in their care as patients. Here's one explanation, though there are several, so you might as well know or might not know.

The reason sick people under a doctor's care are called patients is that the doctor constantly needs to remind himself that he is the only one who is well and in control.

Therefore, he needs patients to take care of the sick people under his care so that when the sick start acting inappropriately, he won't have to get angry with them but rather will be able to find a way to take good care of them in order to get well again. That is why they call them patients.

Dear married people, can you start by looking at your spouse as someone who needs help or is sick, especially sick in their attitude and character, and you as the doctor who can treat him or her well, See him or her as your patient, be patient with their misbehaving attitude, and still find a way, like a doctor, to treat them well.

Marriage needs enough patience with one another for it to work; kindly borrow patience if you do not have enough because you will need it to fix things in your marriage. If we can apply the kind of patience a nursing mother has towards her baby to marriage, I tell you, marriage will be so perfect.

No mother ever throws her baby away because the child pees on her expensive clothes, instead, she will take good care of the child patiently.

The bridegroom vs. the bride

Sometimes, I wonder why the English language uses the words "bridegroom" for the man and "bride" for the woman. In my opinion, though, for men, "bridegroom" is a word that comes from two words, "bride" and "groom." What is the meaning of the word "groom"? It means someone who teaches or trains another person to be perfect at what he or she is doing by themselves.

So as a man or a married man, you are the bridegroom, meaning you are supposed to know enough beforehand so that you can groom your bride in the right direction and to perfection in your marriage. If you read your Bible, Adam already knew enough about things before Eve was created to be his wife. Read what the Bible says below.

"And the Lord God took the man and put him into the garden of Eden to dress it and to keep it. And the Lord God commanded the man, saying, "Of every tree of the garden thou mayest freely eat; but of the tree of the knowledge of good and evil, thou shalt not eat of it; for in the day that thou eatest thereof, thou shalt surely die. And the Lord God said, it is not good that the man should be alone; I will make him a help meet for him. And out of the ground the Lord God formed every beast of the field, and every fowl of the air; and brought them unto Adam to see what he would call them: and whatsoever Adam called every living creature, that was the name thereof. And Adam gave names to all cattle, and to the fowl of the air, and to every beast of the field; but for Adam, there was not found an help meet for him. And the Lord God caused a deep sleep to fall upon Adam, and he

slept; and he took one of his ribs and closed up the flesh instead thereof; and the rib, which the Lord God had taken from man, made him a woman, and he brought her unto the man. And Adam said, "This is now bone of my bones and flesh of my flesh; she shall be called woman because she was taken out of man."
Genesis 2:15-23 KJV
The Bible says Adam was already in the garden, working and giving names to lots of animals; whatever Adam called any animal, that was the name, and God never changed it, meaning Adam knew a lot already before his wife was brought to him.

As a married man, what do you know that you can use to groom your wife in your marriage? And as a single man about to get married, what do you think you can teach or use to groom your wife? So your woman will be the wife of your dreams?

Men take note. Women are created as special, multiplying creatures. This is what I mean: when you give a woman your seed, she gives you a baby; when you show them love, they give you care, respect, and peace.

You give her money, she gives you food, and the rest is up to her. So as a man, mind what you give to your woman; she will multiply it and give it back to you. It was in the lives of women that I understood the meaning. You will reap what you sow a hundredfold.

Whatever you give them, they have the capacity to multiply it and give it back to you. So as a man, when you give hatred, beating, insults, etc., what did you expect she will multiply by it? Men answer this.

Men, you are a bridegroom. You need to consider what you give to your wife. Imagine giving her hatred. Please, what will you get in return after she might have multiplied it? Then those of you who are giving your wife a beating—ah, after she multiplies it for you—the results may be grave for you or her. Mind what you give or teach your woman; as a man, you have the grooming capacity in you to get the best out of her.

As a man, not always giving your wife attention is so bad that was the reason or the only mistake Adam made that landed all of humanity in the mess we are in today.

When Adam neglected to groom his wife, as he was meant to, and instead left her alone, Satan entered and seized control of the grooming session, bringing out something else in Eve. Go through the Bible. The accompanying outcomes were hazardous.

"Now the serpent was more subtle than any beast of the field that the Lord God had made. And he said unto the woman, "Yea, hath God said, you shall not eat of every tree of the garden? And the woman said unto the serpent, "We may eat of the fruit of the trees of the garden; but of the fruit of the tree that is in the midst of the garden, God has said, "Ye shall not eat of it, nor shall ye touch it, lest ye die. And the serpent said unto the woman, "Ye shall not surely die; for God doth know that in the day ye eat thereof, then your eyes shall be opened, and you shall be as gods, knowing good and evil. And when the woman saw that the tree was good for food, that it was pleasant to the eyes, and that it was a tree to be desired to make one wise, she took of the fruit thereof and did eat, and gave also to her husband with her; and he did eat. "And the eyes of them both were opened, and they knew that they were naked, and they sewed fig leaves together and made themselves aprons."

Genesis 3:1–7 KJV

The above Bible verses could lead one to believe that after Adam left for work, the serpent visited the woman to have a conversation. However, verse six seems to indicate that Adam was present when Satan was speaking to her. In any case, Adam neglected to take care of her (grooming), Satan assumed responsibility for it, and Eve produced a different outcome that led to the current state of affairs for all of humanity.

Men need to stay with their wives and do the grooming; this may also be the reason many children are not the biological children of the husband, because you left your grooming to another man who was available to groom her, and when the result came out, she was afraid to lose you, so she hid it from you and pushed it on you just as Eve pushed Adam. As a man, remember this: if you fail to groom her, someone else will avail themselves of the opportunity to do that grooming for you, but the truth is, you will never like or be comfortable with the outcome.

Dealing with conflict and Miscommunication

In your marriage, there will undoubtedly be disagreements and misunderstandings. Any partnership will inevitably include disagreements and miscommunication. But they can be particularly traumatic when they happen in a marriage. This is because problems in a marriage can seem personal because it is a lifetime commitment.

Although handling disagreements and misunderstandings might be challenging, doing so is crucial to the longevity of your marriage. It is critical that you listen to each other's viewpoints and be honest with one another. Additionally, you must be willing to make compromises, even if doing so means sacrificing some of your beliefs and principles, for the marriage to be healthy.

Communicating effectively when you disagree

When you disagree with your spouse, communication is key. Constructively expressing your feelings can help you resolve the disagreement and move on.

However, yelling, insulting, or threatening your spouse will only make things worse. Remember that communication is a two-way street. You need to be willing to listen to your spouse's point of view as well.

This will help you understand where they are coming from, and it may even help you find a solution.

This is also where you need to apply the law of understanding.

The law of understanding says that when one person is standing, the other should try to be under. and when the other person comes down, the other can now be standing while the other is under.

Forgiving and moving on

But don't lose hope—you are not the only one going through this. There will inevitably be difficult times in any marriage, but it is possible to forgive and go on. Though it will require persistence, time, and patience, it is possible to emerge from this experience with a stronger bond than before

.

The first thing you should do is talk to your partner. Discuss what transpired, why it affected you, and how to keep it from happening in the future. It's crucial to express remorse and apologise for whatever you may have done to add to the pain. In order for you two to continue, the other partner must also be prepared to accept the apology.

Then, you need to work on forgiveness. This is easier said than done, but it is essential for moving forward. Forgiveness does not mean forgetting what happened or pretending it did not hurt you.

It just means letting go of the anger and resentment so you can move on. Then focus on rebuilding trust. This will require time and patience, but it is essential for a healthy marriage. Start small by doing things like keeping your promises and being honest with each other.

Over time, you can rebuild the trust that was lost and create a stronger bond than ever before.

In marriage, you need to prepare your mind beforehand. because sometimes your partner will hurt you so much that it seems like you are breathing underwater. and at the end, you will still need to forgive them.

It takes two forgivers to stay in marriage and have a long-lasting marriage. If you do not have the heart to forgive, then you will not be able to stay married, because in marriage, there are lots of rubbish you will need to deal with from your partner, and you will have to take it in and forgive them.

Reconnecting after painful experiences

It is possible to reconnect after painful experiences, but it takes work. You need to be willing to forgive, forget, and move on from the hurt your partner caused you. It is not always easy, but it is worth it.

To reconnect, you need to first identify the issues that caused the pain. Once you know what the issues are, you can start working on fixing them. This may require counselling, therapy, or just open communication with your spouse.

It is important to remember that you are not alone in this. Many couples go through similar experiences and came out stronger from it. With patience and effort, you can too.

Nobody expects to struggle or be hurt in marriage, but sadly, this is a reality for many couples. There are actions you can take to help strengthen your bond and restore trust if you are having trouble getting back together after one of these hurts. I will discuss a few strategies for helping couples reconnect in this chapter:

Setting boundaries for healthy relationships

It is important to set boundaries in any relationship, but it is specially important in marriage. You need to be able to be honest with each other about what is and is not working for you. If you are not careful, it is easy to let your relationship become a source of pain instead of joy.

To avoid this, you need to be willing to have tough conversations with your spouse about what is not working for you. It is not always easy, but it is necessary if you want to have a healthy relationship.

Shared activities

Participating in shared activities can help reunite couples. By doing something together, they can create new memories and concentrate on the positive aspects of their relationship.

It can also be a great way to spend quality time with your family and yourself. Look for activities that the couple enjoys doing together, including going on a stroll, playing a game, preparing and dining meals together, etc. They should also prioritise spending time with each other on a regular basis. They will stay in communication and forge stronger bonds as a result.

Discussing and engaging in activities together might help couples reignite their romance. When a couple interacts openly and honestly, they can share their wants and feelings without fear of criticism. They can also concentrate on the positive aspects of their relationship and create new memories by doing things together. Through strengthening their relationship and rebuilding trust, these two techniques can assist couples who are struggling to reconcile.

Remembering the reasons you fell in love with that person and learning how to express your feelings to them in their "love language" are two more important lessons. When things are tough, extend forgiveness quickly and accept it.

Remember that only God truly understands you; therefore, if you're feeling dissatisfied or frustrated, remember that person isn't there to meet all of your needs. Offer up prayers to him.

Praying and studying the Bible together

Arguments and conflicts are never fun, but they are inevitable when two people are trying to live as one

It is stated that families who pray together stay together; thus, you should never undervalue the importance of family prayer.

God had a purpose and a plan for humanity, and marriage was one of them. Thus, all marriage disputes must be brought back to God in prayer in order to be resolved and have a true, long-lasting solution.

It looks amusing and astonishing how quickly people have kicked God out of their marriages and families, which is one reason Satan is becoming more and more prevalent in marriages and families.

The Bible makes it quite evident that for marriage and families to succeed, God must be at their centre.

"How can two walk together unless they agree?" Amos:3vs3.

The phrase for better or for worse

You might be wondering what could be painful about love in marriage. After all, isn't marriage supposed to be a blissful union of two souls?

Unfortunately, the reality is that even the happiest of marriages can have their share of pain. The phrase "for better or for worse" is not just a sweet sentiment; it is a very real part of being married.

There will be times when your spouse upsets you, when you do not see eye to eye, and when you r plans do not get along. That is normal! What is important is how you handle these disagreements.

You'll be one step closer to having a happy and healthy marriage if you can learn to deal with the difficult aspects of love.

Marriage is both a lovely and a terrible journey when it comes to love. You have the wonderful sensation of being loved and being loved in return. On the one hand, you experience the anguish of feeling deceived, mistreated, and left behind

Accepting the positive and negative aspects of a marriage is essential for its success. You have to acknowledge that love will bring both joy and pain, and you have to be ready to deal with both in your marriage.

Where is that love you once promised your partner?

Love is an amazing emotion. It boosts our self-esteem, fills our lives with joy and contentment, and aids in our development in a variety of other ways. One of the most significant things in life is having the opportunity to experience love, which is a lovely thing.

But marriage is a whole other story. If you're married, you've undoubtedly heard about or experienced the unpleasant aspects of marital love.

It's the difficult moments when you're anxious, irritated, or upset; when your partner minimises or treats you like a nobody; or when you just believe that filing for divorce is your only choice.

However, we frequently ignore several other aspects of love in marriage. Within this book, We shall discuss that

When it comes to sustaining a marriage, it requires a lot of effort and hard work, unlike the excitement of newly wedded who are eager to begin their lives together.

That's right, I said, "hard work." Research has indicated that successful marriages require hard work and dedication, particularly if one hopes to be married for more than 20 years and beyond.

This may come as a surprise to some people, but some are already familiar with what I am saying. Based on the marital struggles of celebrities, it appears that about 50% of American marriages terminate in divorce. It appears that Africa is rapidly approaching that statistic as well.

To make your marriage continue and get through all of the ups and downs, it is of the utmost importance to fully understand the various facets of love in marriage.

The idea of divorce terrifies most people, and not without reason. When you get married, you make a promise to spend the rest of your life with someone else. That is a huge commitment, and one that is supposed to last forever—or at least until death do you part!

But in reality, especially in this new generation, many marriages do not make it to their tenth anniversary. Half of marriages end in divorce by the seventh year of marriage, with some studies putting the number even higher. especially couples who are celebrities, educated, wealthy, and influencers in society.

In contrast to our parents' previous generation, single parenting is now a new and prevalent term in this generation. Nowadays, young women are happy to identify as single mothers, in contrast to the past, when a woman with a child or children without a husband would be embarrassed and even considered a prostitute by society or her community. I'm not arguing that being a single parent is horrible or that it can't happen.

Certain situations, such as having a violent partner, an adulterous partner, or one partner passing away, may reasonably result in solo parenting. However, it is completely out of control to hear young people claim that marriage is a fraud and that, as a result, they will not get married but still have children.

Why are divorce rates higher now than they were in the past? Why do so many deeply in-love couples harbour such animosity towards one another? Even though they were deeply in love with their spouse initially, why did some people's lives change after marriage? We need to come up with solutions to this question, which occasionally bothers me too.

Where is the love that once motivated you to fulfill your role wholeheartedly? The love that, because of your partner, made you restless and sleepless at times? The love that made you feel ill when they didn't visit or call? Do you remember when you used to think every person you saw on the road might be them? The question now is, "Where is that love?"

Have you been reflecting on the state of your marriage? The person who once cared for you deeply now seems like a stranger, leaving you to wonder what went wrong. It's why you sometimes struggle to find answers to your questions. Many people ponder, "Where is the love that was once promised or vowed to me?"

Do you realize that love alone cannot sustain your marriage? There are times when it feels like loving your partner was a mistake, and you wish you could go back in time to change things.

Here's what love sometimes does that makes it feel like a setup: Love brings you together and leads you to marriage, stays with you for a few months or years, and then starts to withdraw. At some point, you both search for love in your marriage and can't find it. But when you look outside your marriage, you see love thriving with other couples. This is when thoughts of cheating creep in, and you start blaming your partner.

Some people begin to think or say that marriage is a scam, while others speak out against it. What they don't realize is... continue in volume 2.

ACKNOWLEDGMENT

I sincerely thank the omnipotent God for bestowing on me the knowledge and divine talent necessary to write this book.

In addition, I want to thank my wife, Queen Eze, for all of her help and inspiration while I was writing this book. I value the contributions you have made.

We appreciate the editing staff's work on the manuscript. My appreciation also extends to Apostle and Mrs. Chuks Eze for all the help you all provided me with during the writing of this book.

I want to express my gratitude to Rev. J. Apkovino, the pastor in charge of the GBM Ajangbadi branch, and to every worker at the Gospel Believers Mission branch in Ajangbadi. I want to express my gratitude to every person in the Christ General Prayer and Evangelical Movement.

I want to express my sincere gratitude to Gen. and Mrs. Ezra J. Jakko, the general overseers of Gospel Believers Mission, as well as to all the ministers and pastors of this great commission, GBM.

ORDER BOOK BY THE AUTHOR

Book Title: **The Spiritual Stamina for End-Time Christian**

Freeson Eze is a teacher of the word of God and a preacher of the gospel. He is passionate about teaching believers how to   live victorious lives in Christ. His teachings are founded on the life-changing truth of the word of God. He hosts a weekly   programme and is the author of The Spiritual Stamina for End-Time Christians. In his quest to impact the Christian culture, he balances his teaching ministry with his involvement in key ministries, including KACY-I, a ministry of evangelism and missions, where he serves as the director.

he is married to Queen Eze, and they are blessed with three boys.

Contact him for conferences, seminars, and any gospel activitie

s.

Email: **marriagemedicine2023@gmail.com**

Freeson U Eze

www.ingramcontent.com/pod-product-compliance
Lightning Source LLC
Chambersburg PA
CBHW050542160726
48003CB00002B/714